D0745808

BLUE BANNER BIOGRAPHY

Jared GOFF

John Bankston

Mitchell Lane

PUBLISHERS

2001 SW 31st Avenue
Hallandale, FL 33009
www.mitchelllane.com

Mitchell Lane
PUBLISHERS

Printing   1   2   3   4   5   6   7   8   9

Blue Banner Biographies

5 Seconds of Summer	Gwen Stefani	Mary-Kate and Ashley Olsen
Aaron Judge	Hope Solo	Megan Fox
Abby Wambach	Ice Cube	Miguel Tejada
Adele	Jamie Foxx	Mike Trout
Alicia Keys	James Harden	Nancy Pelosi
Allen Iverson	Jared Goff	Natasha Bedingfield
Ashanti	Ja Rule	Nicki Minaj
Ashlee Simpson	Jason Derulo	One Direction
Ashton Kutcher	Jay-Z	Orianthi
Avril Lavigne	Jennifer Hudson	Orlando Bloom
Blake Lively	Jennifer Lopez	P. Diddy
Blake Shelton	Jessica Simpson	Peyton Manning
Bow Wow	JJ Watt	Pharrell Williams
Brett Favre	J. K. Rowling	Pit Bull
Britney Spears	John Legend	Prince William
CC Sabathia	Justin Berfield	Queen Latifah
Carrie Underwood	Justin Timberlake	Robert Downey Jr.
Carson Wentz	Kanye West	Ron Howard
Charlie Puth	Kate Hudson	Russell Westbrook
Chris Brown	Keith Urban	Russell Wilson
Chris Daughtry	Kelly Clarkson	Sean Kingston
Christina Aguilera	Kenny Chesney	Selena
Clay Aiken	Ke$ha	Shia LaBeouf
Cole Hamels	Kevin Durant	Shontelle Layne
Condoleezza Rice	Kristen Stewart	Soulja Boy Tell 'Em
Corbin Bleu	Lady Gaga	Stephenie Meyer
Daniel Radcliffe	Lance Armstrong	Taylor Swift
David Ortiz	Leona Lewis	T.I.
David Wright	Le'Veon Bell	Timbaland
Derek Hough	Lindsay Lohan	Tim McGraw
Derek Jeter	LL Cool J	Toby Keith
Drew Brees	Ludacris	Usher
Dwyane Wade	Luke Bryan	Vanessa Anne Hudgens
Eminem	Maren Morris	The Weeknd
Eve	Mariah Carey	Will.i.am
Fergie	Mario	Zac Efron
Flo Rida	Mary J. Blige	

Library of Congress Cataloging-in-Publication Data
Names: Bankston, John, 1974- author.
Title: Jared Goff / by John Bankston.
Description: Hallandale, Florida : Mitchell Lane Publishers, [2019] | Series: Blue Banner Biographies | Includes webography. | Includes bibliographical references and index. | Audience: Ages: 9-13.
Identifiers: LCCN 2018007998| ISBN 9781680202861 (library bound) | ISBN 9781680202878 (ebook)
Subjects: LCSH: Goff , Jared, 1994- —Juvenile literature. | Quarterbacks (Football)—United States—Biography—Juvenile literature. | Los Angeles Rams (Football team : 2016-)—History—Juvenile literature.
Classification: LCC GV939.G625 B36 2018 | DDC 796.332092 [B] —dc23
LC record available at https://lccn.loc.gov/2018007998

ABOUT THE AUTHOR: Born in Boston, Massachusetts, John Bankston began writing professionally while still a teenager. Since then, more than 200 of his articles have been published in magazines and newspapers across the country. He is the author of more than 100 nonfiction books for children and young adults, including Mitchell Lane biographies of Abby Wambach, Kevin Durant, and Selena Gomez. Today he lives in coastal Florida.

PUBLISHER'S NOTE: The following story has been thoroughly researched and to the best of our knowledge represents a true story. While every possible effort has been made to ensure accuracy, the publisher will not assume liability for damages caused by inaccuracies in the data and makes no warranty on the accuracy of the information contained herein. This story has not been authorized or endorsed by Jared Goff.

Blue Banner Biography

Quarterback Jared Goff (16) of the Los Angeles Rams during the game against the Jacksonville Jaguars on October 15, 2017. The Rams defeated the Jaguars 27 to 17.

On the Line

Jared Goff is one of the best up-and-coming quarterbacks in the National Football League (NFL). Yet he almost became an offensive lineman. Offensive linemen protect their team's quarterback and open holes for running backs. The position requires size, strength, and the willingness to hit hard—and be hit hard in return.

It was the first day of practice for youth league football. Jared was seven years old. He ran over to join the linemen. His father didn't think that was the best choice. Jerry Goff usually let his son make up his own mind. This time, however, he spoke up. "It's kind of funny. He was never the biggest kid," he admitted on therams.com. "So he's over there with the linemen and I'm like, 'Man . . . I don't want him to be a lineman.' Because I had just played high school football and I knew his body wasn't meant for that."

Jerry thought it would be better if his son was leading the team. He was good at throwing balls. So he went over to an assistant coach. As he told *The Marin Independent Journal*, he asked, "How about if he tries out

Jared drops back into the pocket during the second quarter of the game against the New Orleans Saints on November 26, 2017. He threw two touchdown passes as the Rams won 26-20.

at quarterback?" The coach wasn't sure. He already had another kid in mind. If Jared wanted to be quarterback, the coach said he needed to work on his footwork. Footwork is very important for quarterbacks.

One important technique of footwork is called the reverse pivot. It is a way of handing the ball off to a running back. So the coach explained that Jared had to learn how to do a reverse pivot. Jerry Goff remembered in the *Journal*, "We got home and he said, 'We're doing the reverse pivot!' So we sat in the backyard and he did the reverse pivot for about 2 hours. And we came back the next day and he's been a quarterback ever since."

Jared has never been afraid to learn new moves. As he was growing up, sometimes his team lost a game. When that happened, Jared didn't blame his teammates. He didn't blame his coaches. Instead, he figured out what he needed to work on. He figured out how to get better.

> *People who know Jared call him laid-back. He's a guy who doesn't get stressed even when things get difficult. Sometimes he'll act goofy to lighten the mood. Sometimes he'll sing songs by his favorite singers.*

People who know Jared call him laid-back. He's a guy who doesn't get stressed even when things get difficult. Sometimes he'll act goofy to lighten the mood. Sometimes he'll sing songs by his favorite singers. But mostly, he'll use the skills he learned growing up in northern California, the son of an athlete whose teammates called him "Robocop."

A baby's first word is usually a simple one. Sometimes it's "Mom." Sometimes it's "Dad." Jared Goff's first word was "ball."

That made sense. His father had been a professional baseball player. In 1990, Jerry Goff played his first Major League Baseball game as a catcher for the Montreal Expos. "I remember a mountain of a man with just a cannon behind the plate," teammate Mike Aldrete told *The Marin Independent Journal*. Goff was 6-foot-3. He weighed over 200 pounds. He was very serious when he played. Some of his teammates nicknamed him after a popular action movie about a robot police officer. They called him "Robocop."

Despite Jerry's talents, he struggled. He was on three teams in six years. Besides the Expos, he played for the Pittsburgh Pirates and Houston Astros. Growing up, he'd been a top baseball and football player at San Rafael High School. The school is located in Marin County, California, across the Golden Gate Bridge from San Francisco. While in high school, he met Jared's mother, Nancy. The two went to college at nearby University of California at Berkeley. They settled in Novato, a town 10 miles from where Jerry grew up.

Jared Thomas Goff was born there on October 14, 1994. His sister Lauren is three years older. Having a dad who was a professional baseball player could be difficult. Major League teams play 162 games during the season. Players spend a lot of time away from home. Not long after Jared was born, Jerry retired from baseball. His last game was in 1996.

Jared and his family during the press conference that introduced him as the Los Angeles Rams first overall draft pick on April 29, 2016. From left to right: Jared, his sister Lauren, and his parents Nancy and Jerry.

Jerry traded his mitt for a hose. He became a firefighter. Some of his fellow firefighters remember Jared when he was little. They all talk about how happy he was—especially when he was playing with a ball. It didn't matter if it was a baseball, a basketball, a football, or a soccer ball.

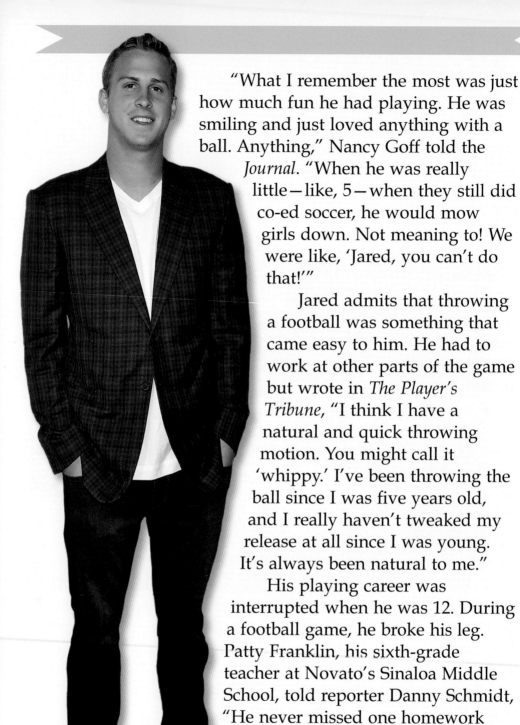

"What I remember the most was just how much fun he had playing. He was smiling and just loved anything with a ball. Anything," Nancy Goff told the *Journal*. "When he was really little—like, 5—when they still did co-ed soccer, he would mow girls down. Not meaning to! We were like, 'Jared, you can't do that!'"

Jared admits that throwing a football was something that came easy to him. He had to work at other parts of the game but wrote in *The Player's Tribune*, "I think I have a natural and quick throwing motion. You might call it 'whippy.' I've been throwing the ball since I was five years old, and I really haven't tweaked my release at all since I was young. It's always been natural to me."

His playing career was interrupted when he was 12. During a football game, he broke his leg. Patty Franklin, his sixth-grade teacher at Novato's Sinaloa Middle School, told reporter Danny Schmidt, "He never missed one homework assignment; not one. He was laid up for a long time, then he was in a wheelchair and on crutches."

Some of Franklin's students left

school for vacations. The teacher told them, "You better come back with your homework, because I've got a kid who broke his leg and didn't miss one assignment."

Jared admits that throwing a football was something that came easy to him.

When he got a little older, Jared started looking at high schools in the area. He wanted to bypass the local public school for a program that produced top athletes in several sports. His cousin Mia Lawrence told the Novato High School paper that Jared chose Marin Catholic because "the sports programs excelled there. When he went to MC, he was not only a football player, but he also played baseball and basketball. He also liked the strong academics they provided and most of his Sinaloa friends were going to MC."

At Marin Catholic, he would have to prove himself to new coaches and new teammates. His parents and friends weren't worried. They knew he was ready.

3 Keeping Cool in High School

At first Marin Catholic head football coach Mazi Moayed wasn't impressed with Jared. On the website for the Los Angeles Rams, he remembered the first time he met Jared. Moayed described him as a "tall, skinny kid who wanted to play quarterback . . . everybody wants to play quarterback." Then he watched Jared play. "You watch him throw the football, and you'd be like, 'Wow, that looked really easy.' Like, you felt like you could do it," Moayed added. "You could tell he was special then."

By the time he was a sophomore, Jared Goff had gotten noticed. It wasn't just for his passing ability. It wasn't just because he was a great athlete. Marin Catholic High School is filled with top athletes. The Wildcats boast 29 sports and 49 individual teams. Nearly every student at the school plays some type of sport. Most teams land near the top in the Marin County Athletic League standings.

Jared had something more than athletic ability. "He's got that calmness, he's got the Joe Coolness,'" Moayed told CBS Sports. "He has that gift."

With so many sports to choose from, Jared played three. As a sophomore, he shared the varsity quarterback spot on the football team. He was also a forward on the basketball team and shortstop on the baseball team. His father admitted that his son might have gotten his athletic talents from him, "but he has some qualities that I wish I had when I was playing," Jerry Goff said on Sports Stars of Tomorrow. "He doesn't get too rattled. He doesn't get too high, he doesn't get too low." It is the perfect way to be a successful quarterback. And at Marin Catholic, Jared Goff was definitely a successful quarterback.

Jared scores a touchdown in the first quarter of the CIF Division 1 California State Football Championship game between Marin Catholic and Madison on December 15, 2012.

During his three years as varsity quarterback, he threw for over 7,000 yards and 93 touchdowns. His team only lost four games. Every year, the team made it to the Marin

County Championship. His junior year alone he threw 44 touchdowns. He realized he might have a shot at being a college football player.

"I had a pretty good year," he remembered on therams.com, "a bunch of touchdowns and not many interceptions and we were really good. I had some pretty good receivers around me that year and that's when I kind of knew I could do it, started getting some interest."

As a senior, Jared took his team all the way to the state championship. Traveling to Southern California in 2012, the Wildcats faced the San Diego Madison Warhawks. Early on, the Wildcats posted 21 unanswered points. But Jared was a big target. By then he was 6-foot-4 and weighed almost 200 pounds. Again and again Jared got sacked. In the end, Madison eked out a 38–35 victory. Madison coach Rick Jackson told *UT Preps*, "That quarterback was unbelievable. Phenomenal."

Despite the defeat, Jared already had a plan for college. To fulfill it, he would have to give up the final months of his senior year.

Too Much to Bear

As a senior, Jared had a lot of choices. Schools like Boise State, Fresno State, and Stanford University recruited him. He took his time and considered all his options. In the end, it was an easy decision. He would play for the University of California at Berkeley. In sports, the school is usually referred to as California, or even just Cal. It was the same school his parents had attended.

"We were so happy—I was so happy. It's unreal, it really is unreal, as a mom who went to school there, to have your son then deciding that he's going to play there," Nancy Goff told therams.com. "And, hopefully, be the starting quarterback at Cal. I watched Jerry play there. So to be back on that field, Memorial Stadium, with Jared starting was unreal."

The school is part of the Pac-12 Conference. It is made up of teams in Washington, Oregon, California, Arizona, Utah, and Colorado. Earning a scholarship to a school in the Pac-12 is a big accomplishment. For Jared, it meant giving something back to his parents. He felt they had done so much for him. Now they wouldn't have to spend money on his tuition. Plus, the school was close to home. They could easily attend all his home games.

There was one problem. The school wanted him to start practicing in the spring. That meant instead of finishing his senior year at Marin Catholic, he had to enroll at California so he could take part in the football team's spring training workouts. Marin Catholic wasn't willing to let anything slide. Jared had to take online classes. He had to take summer school classes. He made it work.

Defensive tackle Elijah Qualls, defensive end Garrett Hughes, and Jared congratulate one another at the Semper Fidelis All-American Bowl on January 4, 2013. The game featured many of country's top prep football players.

By the fall of 2013, he was ready to begin playing. First-year college football players are usually "redshirted." This means they can practice with the team but can't play in games. Jared wasn't redshirted. In 2013, he became the first true freshman starting quarterback in Cal history.

He did not have a great first year. Before he even started, the coach who'd recruited him was fired. The new coach, Sonny Dykes, watched video of Jared playing. He was not impressed. Then he saw him play. "If you could design a quarterback, it would look a lot like Jared Goff," Dykes later told reporter Sean Wagner-McGough.

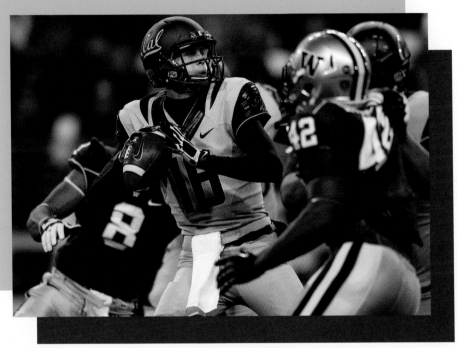

Jared passes against the Washington Huskies on October 26, 2013. Though he completed 32 passes for a total of 336 yards, the Golden Bears lost 41-17.

Dykes kept Jared as starter. Fans often questioned that choice. In his very first game, the Golden Bears only scored 16 points. Their opponent, Oregon, scored 55! Jared was benched in the first quarter.

The team only won a single game that season, against low-ranked Portland State. In 10 of their 11 losses, the score wasn't even close. "I don't think people understand

Linebacker Christian French of the Oregon Ducks sacks Jared during a game in his sophomore year. Jared passed for 360 yards as Cal lost a 59-41 shootout.

how difficult that was for an 18-year-old kid," Jerry Goff told ESPN in 2017. "Unless you've been through it, you don't know how hard that is."

Dykes told *The Los Angeles Times* in 2016. "We threw that poor kid to the wolves his first year. I can remember we were having issues with one of our players. I was like, 'Look, I've had 15 conversations with you about an issue. I've never had one conversation with Jared Goff or his parents about an issue since he's been here. . . . He's going

to be a first-round player [in the NFL Draft], and you're a walk-on.'"

Even when the team was losing, Jared tried to keep it light. He did everything he could to remind the other players that it was a game, it was supposed to be fun. If that didn't work, he'd dance around to Taylor Swift or Justin Bieber. "He totally likes Justin Bieber," his sister Lauren told *The Los Angeles Times* in August, 2016. "He unashamedly likes pop music, and I do too."

Jared spent the off-season improving. He trained hard in the weight room. He studied the playbook. He watched game video. Before his sophomore year, he was named team captain. All his hard work paid off. The team improved to 5–7. Jared threw 35 touchdown passes.

In 2015, Jared led his team to an 8-5 record. He also set Pac-12 records with 4,719 passing yards and 43 touchdown passes. He earned first-team All-Pac-12 honors. By now, he held 26 school records, including most career passing yards, total offense, and touchdown passes.

Friends remember how he found silly ways to celebrate. After one win, he invited the school's marching band

> **Jared spent the off-season improving.**

to play at the off-campus house he shared with several teammates. The band performed the Cal fight song. It was three a.m.

In December, the Golden Bears competed in the Armed Forces Bowl against Air Force. Jared threw for 467 yards and six touchdowns as Cal romped to a 55–36 triumph. It was California's first postseason win in seven years. Fans chanted "One more year!" After the game, Dykes admitted, "I was chanting that too."

Head coach Troy Calhoun of the Air Force Falcons congratulates Jared and head coach Sonny Dykes after the Golden Bears beat the Falcons in the Armed Forces Bowl.

Jared knew he had a tough choice to make. There were good reasons to keep playing his senior year. Yet he was already getting attention from NFL teams. Playing college sports is risky. Top athletes often get injured playing. That hurts their chance of playing for the pros. Jared decided to enter the NFL draft.

5

To Live and Play in L.A.

The Los Angeles Rams needed a quarterback. After 21 years in St. Louis, Missouri, the team was moving back to California. Getting a star quarterback was the first step to becoming a top team. General Manager Les Snead started looking at the best college quarterbacks. He flew to Northern California, hoping to watch Jared practice. Unfortunately, it was supposed to rain the next day. Snead looked at the weather forecast. He found several brief periods of clearing and suggested those. In an interview with *Sports Illustrated* in 2017, he remembered what Goff told him. "We're going at 8:30 a.m. . . . And I hope it rains."

Jared got his wish. Snead made up his mind as he watched Goff play well despite the bad weather. The Rams would do whatever they had to in order to make sure that Jared was their quarterback.

There was a problem. The Rams only had the 15th pick in the 2016 draft. They knew Jared would be long gone by that time. So they engineered a deal with the Tennessee Titans, who had the first overall pick. The Rams traded Tennessee a first-round pick, two second-round picks, and a third-round pick in 2016, plus a first and third in 2017.

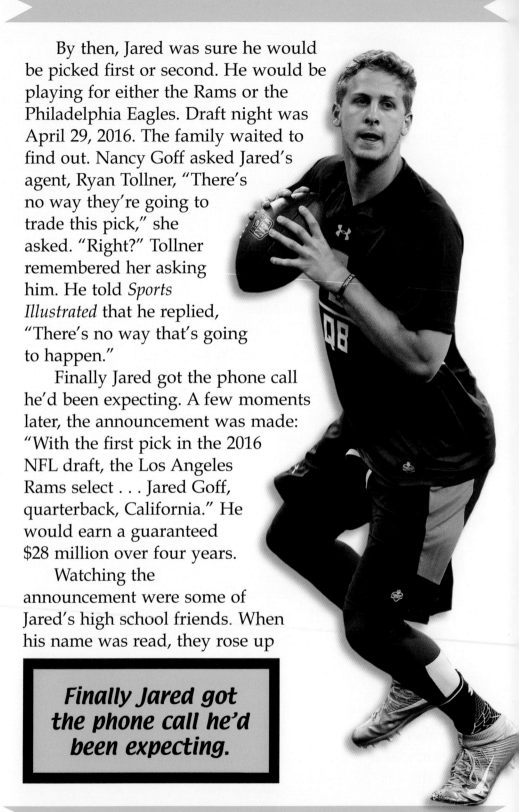

By then, Jared was sure he would be picked first or second. He would be playing for either the Rams or the Philadelphia Eagles. Draft night was April 29, 2016. The family waited to find out. Nancy Goff asked Jared's agent, Ryan Tollner, "There's no way they're going to trade this pick," she asked. "Right?" Tollner remembered her asking him. He told *Sports Illustrated* that he replied, "There's no way that's going to happen."

Finally Jared got the phone call he'd been expecting. A few moments later, the announcement was made: "With the first pick in the 2016 NFL draft, the Los Angeles Rams select . . . Jared Goff, quarterback, California." He would earn a guaranteed $28 million over four years.

Watching the announcement were some of Jared's high school friends. When his name was read, they rose up

Finally Jared got the phone call he'd been expecting.

and cheered. Cameron Croteau graduated from Marin Catholic the same year as Jared. He told *Sports Illustrated*, "We were pretty anxious and nervous, sweating and hoping for the best. And then we just went absolutely nuts. We basically lost our minds."

Rams head coach Jeff Fisher told ESPN, "Jared has a skill set that is special. Once you look at his body of work in the red zone, it's impressive. He keeps drives alive. Nothing is too big for him."

Jared signs autographs after a Rams' preseason workout in 2016, his rookie year.

Jared had to wait to be a starter. He sat on the bench for the team's first nine games. He finally started on November 20 against the Miami Dolphins. The Rams lost that game, and the next six as well. Fisher was fired even before the season ended.

Jared tries to elude Spencer Paysinger of the Miami Dolphins during his first game as a starter. Miami scored with 36 seconds remaining to spoil his debut, 14-10.

Jared had only completed slightly more than half his passes. Even worse, he kept getting hit. When a quarterback has the ball, the other team wants to stop him from completing a pass. One of the best ways to do that is to tackle him. Sometimes a quarterback is sacked because his offensive line doesn't protect him. Sometimes he doesn't pass the ball fast enough. Both things happened in Goff's first pro season. By the end of the year he had been sacked 26 times!

Both Snead and the team's new coach, Sean McVay, were impressed by how Jared dealt with the situation. He didn't blame Fisher or his linemen. McVay told writer Pete Prisco, "he was supposed to still be at Cal, it was a lot to handle. When you are a young quarterback, how you handle the tough stuff says a lot about you, and I think he did a good job."

> **McVay had a plan. He would make sure Jared had better protection so he had more time to pass.**

McVay had a plan. He would make sure Jared had better protection so he had more time to pass. Sometimes teams spend money on a quarterback but don't improve the offensive line. Then the quarterback gets hurt. "If you go get that [star] quarterback, get him some help," Tennessee Titans offensive coordinator Terry Robiske told *The Wall Street Journal*.

McVay did exactly that. He added two veteran offensive linemen: left tackle Andrew Whitworth and center John Sullivan. He also added three wideouts: Sammy Watkins, Robert Woods, and third-round draft pick Cooper Kupp.

After his hard rookie season, Jared took a vacation with friends from high school. When he returned, he started training with Adam Dedeaux, who had worked with players like Tom Brady and Matt Ryan.

Rams' head coach Sean McVay talks to Jared before the game against the San Francisco 49ers on September 21, 2017. Jared's three touchdown passes helped Los Angeles win, 41-39.

They worked together over 30 times. They focused on Jared's footwork and on the one thing he hadn't had to work on: his throwing. He

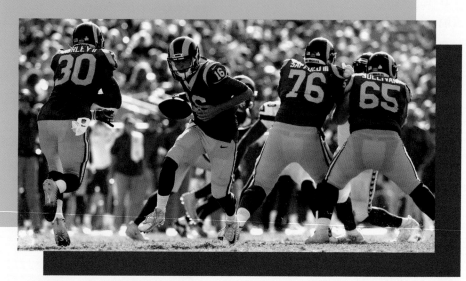

Jared fakes a handoff to Todd Gurley (30) as Rodger Saffold (76) and John Sullivan (65) block during the second half of a game against the Seattle Seahawks on October 8, 2017. Seattle won, 16-10.

concentrated on driving passes with his body rather than with his arm. He shortened his motion.

Jared also studied the playbook every chance he got. He hit the gym. Over the summer, he added ten pounds of muscle.

On the Fourth of July in 2017, he and his friends celebrated by playing touch football on the sand outside their rented house in Newport Beach. His sister Lauren told *Sports Illustrated* that "His energy was noticeably different this offseason. He seemed more at ease."

> **Jared also studied the playbook every chance he got.**

He carried that ease with him as he started his second season with the Rams. The team beat the Indianapolis Colts in their first game, 46-9. Jared passed for 306 yards. That performance set the tone for the rest of the season. Jared started every game as Los Angeles finished 11–5 and won the NFC West. It was the team's first winning season since 2003. McVay was named Coach of the

Year. Unfortunately, the Rams struggled in the first round of the playoffs. Atlanta defeated them by a score of 26–13.

Jared was named to the Pro Bowl. That is the first in what is likely to be a long string of honors for this brilliant young player. For Jared Goff, there is never a reason to doubt. "You have to believe in yourself," he told CBS Sports. "It's the most important thing. I have a tough time losing confidence in myself."

Guard Trai Turner (70) of the Carolina Panthers, center Travis Fredrick (72) of the Dallas Cowboys, and guard T.J. Lang of the Detroit Lions prepare to block for Jared in the 2018 NFL Pro Bowl Game. Though Jared's West team lost 24-23, he was the team's leading passer with 10 completions.

1994 Jared Goff is born on October 14 in Novato, California, to Jerry and Nancy Goff.

2002 Jared begins playing quarterback in the Marin County Youth League.

2010 Starts as quarterback at Marin Catholic High School.

2013 Graduates from Marin Catholic High School; begins attending University of California Berkeley and becomes the first true freshman starting quarterback in school history.

2015 Jared is named to the All-Pac-12 first team.

2016 Enters the NFL draft and the Los Angeles Rams make him the first overall selection.

2017 Jared is named to the Pro Bowl as Rams win NFC West with an 11–5 record.

CAREER STATS

Year	Team	PA	PC	Y	TD
2013	UC Berkeley	530	320	3,508	18
2014	UC Berkeley	509	316	3,973	35
2015	UC Berkeley	529	341	4,714	43
2016	Los Angeles Rams	205	112	1,089	5
2017	Los Angeles Rams	477	296	3,804	28

PA = passes attempted, PC = passes completed, Y = yardage, TD = touchdowns

FIND OUT MORE

Books

Editors of Sports Illustrated Kids. *Football: Then to WOW! New York: Sports Illustrated, 2014.*

Gramling, Gary. *The Football Fanbook: Everything You Need to Become a Gridiron Know-it-All*. New York: Sports Illustrated, 2017.

On the Internet

The Los Angeles Rams
    http://www.therams.com

Jared Goff
    https://www.foxsports.com/nfl/jared-goff-player-stats

WORKS CONSULTED

Periodicals

Beaton, Andrew. "Titans Show How to Build Around a Quarterback." *The Wall Street Journal*, November 16, 2017.

Bishop, Greg. "Jared Goff Is Thriving at the Center of Les Snead's Two-Phase Plan." *Sports Illustrated*, October 24, 2017. https://www.si.com/nfl/2017/10/24/jared-goff-los-angeles-rams-les-snead-sean-mcvay

Brown, Daniel. "Rise to Stardom: Jared Goff Keeps Marin Ties Close as NFL Draft Day Arrives." *The Marin Independent Journal*, April 27, 2016. http://www.marinij.com/article/NO/20160427/NEWS/160429835

Carpenter, Jason. "Losing Local Athletes." *Novato High School Swarm*. http://www.novatoswarm.com/losing-local-athletes.html

Farmer, Sam. "Jared Goff's Laid-back Nature, Blue-collar Work Ethic could be a First-class Ticket to the top of NFL draft." *Los Angeles Times*, April 24, 2016. http://www.latimes.com/sports/nfl/la-sp-nfl-draft-goff-20160424-story.html

"Jared Goff Throws Six Touchdown Passes in Armed Forces Victory Over Air Force." *The Seattle Times*, December 29, 2015. https://www.seattletimes.com/sports/other-sports/jared-goff-of-california-throws-6-touchdown-passes-in-armed-forces-bowl-victory-over-air-force/

Klemko, Roberto. "They Tried to Make Jared Goff Sweat." *Sports Illustrated*, May 3, 2016. https://www.si.com/mmqb/2016/05/03/jared-goff-los-angeles-rams-nfl-draft-night

Schmidt, Danny. "Marin Friends Rejoice as Jared Goff is Taken No. 1 by the L.A. Rams." *The Marin Independent Journal*, April 28, 2016. http://www.marinij.com/article/NO/20160428/SPORTS/160429799

"Who is Jared Goff? Dog lover, 'Cheesy Pop' listener, No. 1 NFL draft pick." *Los Angeles Times*, August 22, 2016. http://www.latimes.com/sports/rams/la-sp-rams-goff-family-20160822-snap-story.html

Web Sites

"Congratulations to Our #1'S, Nicholas Kwok '12 & Jared Goff '13,'" *Marin Catholic News and Events*, May 7, 2016. https://www.marincatholic.org/page/news?pk=852753&fromId=153532

Goff, Jared. "Training Day." *The Players' Tribune*, April 26, 2016. https://www.theplayerstribune.com/jared-goff-cal-berkeley-2016-nfl-draft-photo-gallery/

Gonzalez, Alden. "Jared Goff's Father: 'He's going to be great. He's never not been.'" ESPN, August 1, 2017. http://www.espn.com/blog/los-angeles-rams/post/_/id/34513/jared-goffs-father-hes-going-to-be-great-hes-never-not-been

Maffei, John. "Madison Gets Best of Marin Catholic QB." *U-T Preps*, December 15, 2012. http://hs.utpreps.com/news_article/show/202739?referrer_id=599134

Prisco, Pete. "Jared Goff is Out to Flip the Script that He's Another Hollywood Flop." CBS Sports, August 16, 2017. https://www.cbssports.com/nfl/news/jared-goff-is-out-to-flip-the-script-that-hes-another-hollywood-flop/

"Quarterback Footwork for Handoffs." y-coach.com-forum, August 26, 2004. http://www.y-coach.com/forums/index.php?/topic/373-quarterback-footwork-for-handoffs/

Simmons, Myles. "A Familiar Position for Jared Goff." therams.com, July 27, 2017. http://www.therams.com/news-and-events/article-feature/A-Familiar-Position-For-Jared-Goff/5fc43c88-b06a-4c94-86e9-3be059e0c619

Wagner-McGough, Sean. "How Cal is Developing Jared Goff into the Next Great NFL Hope." CBS Sports, September 11, 2015. https://www.cbssports.com/college-football/news/how-cal-is-developing-jared-goff-into-the-next-great-nfl-quarterback-hope/

Video

"Jared Goff—Marin Catholic Quarterback: Highlights/Interview," Sports Stars of Tomorrow/ Gameday Sports Stars. January 7, 2013. https://www.youtube.com/watch?v=BNy-Ne-KEok

INDEX